Evening

at the

Talk House

OTHER WORKS BY WALLACE SHAWN

SCREENPLAYS:
My Dinner with André
by Wallace Shawn and André Gregory
Marie and Bruce
by Wallace Shawn and Tom Cairns
A Master Builder
based on *The Master Builder* by Henrik Ibsen

TRANSLATIONS/ADAPTATIONS:
The Mandrake by Niccolò Machiavelli
A Master Builder by Henrik Ibsen
The Threepenny Opera by Bertolt Brecht

OPERA LIBRETTI:
In the Dark, music by Allen Shawn
The Music Teacher, music by Allen Shawn

ESSAYS:
Essays

PLAYS:
The Hotel Play
Our Late Night
A Thought in Three Parts
Marie and Bruce
Aunt Dan and Lemon
The Fever
The Designated Mourner
Grasses of a Thousand Colors

Evening

at the

Talk House

Wallace Shawn

THEATRE COMMUNICATIONS GROUP
NEW YORK
2017

The publication of *Evening at The Talk House*, by Wallace Shawn, through TCG's Book Program, is made possible in part by the New York State Council on the Arts with the support of Governor Andrew Cuomo and the New York State Legislature.

TCG books are exclusively distributed to the book trade by Consortium Book Sales and Distribution.

Library of Congress Control Numbers:
2016040003 (print) / 2016053904 (ebook)
ISBN 978-1-55936-520-8 (paperback) / ISBN 978-1-55936-860-5 (ebook)

Book design and composition by Lisa Govan
Cover design by Mark Melnick
Cover images: Getty Images (brick wall); iStockphoto (plaque);
Getty Images (woman's hand)

First Edition, January 2017

To
Jenny Eisenberg
Nell Eisenberg
Lev Eisenberg
Annie Shawn
Harold Shawn
Noa Shawn

. . . after very bitter struggle, a new land,
with cool mornings and peaceful evenings . . .

—FENSTER, *THE BROOK*

Evening

at the

Talk House

Production History

Evening at The Talk House received its world premiere at the Dorfman Theatre at the National Theatre in London (Rufus Norris, Director of the National Theatre; Lisa Burger, Executive Director), in association with Scott Rudin, on November 24, 2015. The production was directed by Ian Rickson. The design was by the Quay Brothers, the costume design was by Soutra Gilmour, the lighting design was by Neil Austin, the music design was by Stephen Warbeck, the sound design was by Ian Dickinson, and the movement direction was by Maxine Doyle; the stage manager was David Marsland. The cast was:

ROBERT	Josh Hamilton
NELLIE	Anna Calder-Marshall
JANE	Sinéad Matthews
TED	Stuart Milligan
ANNETTE	Naomi Wirthner
BILL	Joseph Mydell
TOM	Simon Shepherd
DICK	Wallace Shawn

Evening at The Talk House received its U.S. premiere at the The New Group (Scott Elliott, Artistic Director; Adam Bernstein, Executive Director) in New York on January 31, 2017. The production was directed by Scott Elliott. The set design was by Derek McLane, the costume design was by Jeff Mahshie, and the lighting design was by Jennifer Tipton; the production stage manager was Valerie A. Peterson. The cast was:

ROBERT	Matthew Broderick
NELLIE	Jill Eikenberry
JANE	Annapurna Sriram
TED	John Epperson
ANNETTE	Claudia Shear
BILL	Michael Tucker
TOM	Larry Pine
DICK	Wallace Shawn

Characters

ROBERT	perhaps sixties, tall, attractive
NELLIE	perhaps sixties, thin
JANE	perhaps early thirties, thin
TED	perhaps fifties, not tall
ANNETTE	perhaps fifties, not thin
BILL	perhaps fifties, not tall
TOM	perhaps sixties, tall, attractive
DICK	perhaps sixties, not thin

Note to anyone directing this play: While writing the play, I imagined that the characters had certain characteristics. This is how I imagined the characters. Obviously, it's up to you to decide whether or not you want the age and appearance of all the characters to conform exactly to what I say in the list above, because you may have good reasons in certain cases for making a different choice. In London in 2015 and New York in 2017, we sometimes ignored the suggestions above.

The central meeting room of The Talk House, an old-fashioned, understated small club. Several armchairs, some facing away from us. There is a bar, with various bottles, where guests can refill their drinks. Robert is a tall, attractive man, perhaps in his sixties.

ROBERT

I got a call from Ted the other night. That was a surprise. It had probably been five or six years since I'd heard from Ted. Of course, I'd never really— Well, I was about to say I'd never really known Ted that well—but then who *have* I known well, when you get right down to it, come to think of it?—so I guess I won't say that. To "know someone well"—I mean, that's a phrase from another time. That's an idiotic phrase. Who have I known well? I haven't known anyone well. But at any rate, Ted, you see, had composed

7

some incidental music for a play I'd written a dozen years ago or so called *Midnight in a Clearing with Moon and Stars*— quite nice music, actually—and at that time, you see, when theater played a somewhat larger part in the life of our city than it does now, Ted had been rather successful, he drove a rather nice car, he wore some pretty good-looking jackets and shirts, he was doing all right, but as far as I'd heard, his fortunes had declined, so it was in a way rather touching that he wanted to gather together some of the old gang from *Midnight*, as we called it, to commemorate the tenth anniversary of its opening night, a date I myself would never otherwise have noticed. You see, according to Ted, that play had apparently been a very happy experience for all concerned. I mean, that's what he said, and it was nice to hear that, I guess, and I suppose I'd had a nice time, myself, relatively speaking, during the production of that play. Certainly it would be reasonable to call it, from many points of view, my best play, if one bothers to get involved in those invidious comparisons.

Like all my plays, *Midnight* was set in a period that to a lot of people seemed vaguely medieval, but I always explained that really most of my plays took place in a sort of imaginary kingdom that predated history altogether or stood to one side of it, at any rate. *Midnight in a Clearing with Moon and Stars* told the story of a powerful king, his loyal sons, and a princess, but actually the central figure was a sort of independent knight who lived in an enormous forest quite near the area ruled over by the king. Well—in any case, the play hadn't been terribly well liked by the public, and it wasn't a success, but quite a few people had enjoyed it quite a bit, including, interestingly, a certain Mr. Ackerley, who not long afterwards began to take a more and more prominent place in our national life, which, I'd have to admit, was not unhelpful to me when certain lovely prizes were awarded several years later, after I'd moved into the more congenial form of writing that sustains me today. Of course there are quite a few people who look back lovingly and longingly on the era of Walter Barclay in which that play was written, but you can put me down as a bit of a skeptic on that. I mean, was that really such a happy time? I'm not so sure. Certainly we can all agree that Walter Barclay was a very nice fellow, and Mr. Ackerley, as we know, has a cruel side, more and more in evidence, one could say, but how do these personal traits translate themselves into nation-wide happiness or unhappiness, or do they, you see? I think that's the question that's sometimes ignored. Mind you, I keep my views of Ackerley to myself, as most people obviously do if they have any brains. Walls have ears—as do floors, ceilings, windows, doors, plates, cups, spoons, forks, and come to think of it, other human beings, if we're compiling a list. In any case, the alternation between Mr. Ackerley and our sneaky friend Mr. Rodman seems to work rather well, I feel, and I'm certainly not going to complain because statistics say that the theatergoing impulse has declined substantially since Walter Barclay took his last breath—or had it taken from him, if you believe those theories. A decline in the theatergoing impulse could in a way be seen as a small price to pay for the rather substantial benefit derived from entering into an era that quite a few people would describe as much more tranquil and much more agreeable than the one that preceded it. And the horrible truth, if I dare to say this, is that although I had some fairly nice times, some pretty good moments, putting on my plays—well, if pressed to the wall, I'd have to say that theater for me eventually came to seem like a rather narrow corner, a rather distasteful little corner of the world in which to spend my life—I came to feel that it was a corner of the world that I honestly wouldn't mind leaving and whose general decline I was not in my heart of hearts terribly saddened about. Because, what exactly *was* "theater," really, when you actually thought about it? You'd have to say that it was utterly and irreducibly about a small group of humans sitting and staring at another small group of humans—an animal process—an animal process that completely lacked art, not to mention, for my money, charm, and that was fundamentally no less mindless than what dogs do or what cows do, an animal business of sniffing and staring. No one really cared about the sound track to the event, the words that were spoken—the writer's role was just to choose whether the cows on stage said "Moo" or whether they said "Moo moo." And when I was young, that was all right with me. When I was young, I myself was still in love with the experience of sitting in a darkened theater and staring at the stage, and that was why I devoted all those years to putting on plays. I loved to *look* at them, I loved to stare at the actors and even the scenery they were placed in. In other words, well—I was unfailingly excited—one could even say awestruck—by the sight of an enormous stage, filled and over-filled with enormous shaggy trees rising as high as one could see—and even higher than one could see—and lit by beautiful, suffusing, milky moonlight . . . And then into that milky moonlight, people would stride, with glinting and flashing swords and maces—tall, gorgeous people in flowing robes of blue and red—you know, and I loved the scantily clad nymphs and the magnificent beards of the virile young men. I loved all of that. And sure—part of the pleasure I took in watching those figures was that their very manner, their bearing, so often reflected certain extremely noble but at the same time perennially threatened ideals that I greatly admired then—and still do: self-sacrifice, first of all, I suppose; courage—or heroism on a field of battle, if that was the venue; loyalty; the instantaneous, repeated decision to choose suffering in preference to dishonor. The power and magnificence of the body, I suppose, when inspired into action. And in a way one could laugh, but I still like to think that what we do each week on *Tony and Company*, admittedly in an entirely different style, presents some of the same ideals in a more contemporary package in each little thirty-minute segment. Tony—particularly as Tom plays him, of course—is understandable, he's human, he has his failings and his weaknesses, but he's fundamentally a good person who's guided by the same principles that inspired some of the characters in my plays—he's a person who's prepared to fight when necessary to defend his friends. Or that's how I would see it.

But at any rate, when I asked Ted where he thought we should hold our great anniversary celebration, he replied, "Why, The Talk House of course!" The Talk House? My God, The Talk House, that almost-legendary, wonderfully quiet and genteel club, known far and wide at one time for its delicious and generously sized snacks, some of them pleasantly sautéed, some delightfully freezing cold, all rather charming and unexpected—The Talk House, rather like my own play, had fallen completely out of my mind in recent years, and I was shocked to learn, quite frankly, that it still even existed. But of course it was the perfect place for us all to gather, because during the run of *Midnight*, many of us had gone there after the show almost every night to have a few drinks and enjoy a large or small dinner made up out of some alluring combination of attractive snacks. And of course everyone loved the incredibly kind matron who managed the place, Nellie, a very intelligent, very sensible, rather innocent woman, who always made me feel, when I would walk in the door and see her standing there, that I was a young student just starting out at a rather good school where I could feel quite confident I was going to be well taken care of.

(Nellie—thin, perhaps in her sixties—appears behind Robert and begins arranging the room.)

Nellie of course was assisted by Jane, who ten years ago had been a very young aspiring actress. As I happened to know, Jane had left The Talk House not too long after the days of *Midnight*, but unfortunately she hadn't had great luck as a performer, and I wasn't terribly surprised to learn from Ted that she'd eventually returned to her old job with Nellie.

(After a moment, Jane—perhaps early thirties, thin—appears, and begins to help Nellie. Nellie and Jane wear uniforms. Then we see Ted—perhaps in his fifties, not tall—come in the door and greet Nellie and Jane.)

These days Ted made a living writing advertising music whenever—to use his words—"something came up for which a more old-fashioned composer seemed appropriate." At any rate, that's how he put it to me.

(Annette—perhaps in her fifties, not thin—comes in and greets Nellie, Jane, and Ted.)

Annette had been our wardrobe supervisor on *Midnight*— that was her official title—but to many of us she'd been a special friend and confidante as well, because in stressful circumstances one could always count on Annette to stay pleasant and calm—a soothing presence. She now did private tailoring and repairs for various wealthy clients—a rather unstable mode of existence, as Ted explained it to me.

(Bill—perhaps in his fifties, not tall—enters and greets the others.)

Bill, our resourceful producer, was actually doing quite nicely these days. He'd become a talent agent, and was now quite well known and highly regarded in his new profession.

(Tom—perhaps in his sixties, tall and attractive—arrives and greets the others.)

And then of course there was Tom, the gorgeous and resplendent Tom, the star ten years ago of the not-terribly-successful theatrical masterpiece *Midnight in a Clearing with Moon and Stars*, and currently the star of the *unbelievably* successful television masterpiece *Tony and Company*, for which I've had the honor for the last many years of laboring as head writer, story editor, chief word-wrangler, or whatever you'd want to call me.

(Nellie, Jane, Ted, Annette, Bill, and Tom go off together as Robert continues to speak to the audience.)

At any rate, as the author of the immortal dramatic work that we were gathering to celebrate, I considered it my prerogative to show up a fashionable twelve minutes late, and as the others had all wandered off into the library before I arrived, I didn't see anyone in the club's main meeting room when I came into it, and so I decided to begin my evening by experiencing the men's room briefly. When I stepped outside of the men's room a moment later, I hovered for a short time in the midst of a sort of small glade of armchairs in my usual rather confused state of suspended animation, looking this way and that, when all of a sudden a rather large blurry figure quite unexpectedly rose up from one of the armchairs to greet me. Dick.

(Dick—perhaps in his sixties, not thin—stands up out of one of the armchairs. He slowly makes his way across the stage to Robert.)

I was taken aback—shocked. First of all, Dick was one of the last people on earth I'd ever expected to see in my life again. Quite a famous actor some decades before—his face, wearing the trademark mustache of his character, "Chico," had adorned the front of coffee cans for all the many years that *Carlos and Jenny* had been the nation's most beloved show—he'd fallen on hard times after the show ended and had become, by the time we all knew him, a sort of rather pitiful theatrical hanger-on. Eventually he'd sort of slipped out of town without anyone's noticing, and I'd always assumed he'd gone to some quiet, small city, gotten sick, and died. Second of all—my God—his appearance had horribly changed. He was much heavier, almost fat, and he was

dressed in the most hideous sort of pajama-like sports out-
fit, this once rather elegant man who'd actually been sort
of a famous dandy in his day. And then the other thing was
that Dick's cheeks and nose seemed definitely bruised, and
his mouth too seemed to have been hurt somehow and was
crusted, perhaps, with a bit of dried blood. In fact, one could
hardly credit the fact that a person who looked the way he
did was standing in the well-known rose-colored parlor of
this rather refined, rather lady-like club. In other words, this
was not quite The Talk House as I recalled it from days gone
by. As I stood there flabbergasted, trying to get my bearings,
I also began to surmise that, to top it all off, Dick might be
drunk, in fact he looked as if he'd been drunk for days, or
if he wasn't drunk, then he somehow seemed to be neuro-
logically impaired or damaged in some way. He took a step
toward me slowly and looked me in the eye. "Robert," he
said and stared unwaveringly. Then he raised his hand as if
to hit me, and then he stumbled backwards. I held him by the
forearm to stabilize him and said, "Good to see you, Dick."

DICK

Robert.

*(He raises his hand, stumbles backward, and Robert holds his
forearm.)*

ROBERT

Good to see you, Dick.

DICK

Well, well. Just great to see *you* . . .

ROBERT

I mean, really, Dick, this is amazing, how are you?

DICK

I'm absolutely fine. Very very well. *(A slight pause)* What? Oh—this? *(Pointing to his face)* Well! No—I— *(Somewhat more quietly and confidentially)* No, don't worry about that! I *was* beaten, rather recently, by some friends, but you see, I actually enjoyed it very much, in the end. Really, it was great. No—I loved it! In fact, you should try it some time, Robert. It's not what you think. It was quite fun, I'm serious.

ROBERT

My God, what happened?

DICK

Well, it was a short battering. You know. Informal. A small group of my friends—we met, you know, and they just said, Dick, you see, you're getting a bit close to being "grr— grr—grr—" *(He covers his mouth and makes a weird animal sound, miming odd animal-like behavior)* so we have to "ergh" *(Miming some punches)* —and we have to "ergh" *(More mimed blows)* —and maybe a bit of "ergh" . . . *(Mimed kicks)*

ROBERT

You mean they—?—

DICK

They were right, obviously. I was getting to the point where I was about to cross a line, and this was sort of a case of, "Stop! Go back a few steps!" You know, that sort of thing.

(Robert stares at Dick.)

ROBERT

Crossing a line? But, Dick—my God, you were—you were always such a quiet, well-behaved little bastard when I knew you, Dick.

DICK

I still am! *(He laughs loudly)* But that's what I find myself saying every day. *I* haven't changed. Everything *else* has changed. Do you know what I mean? Why are things different? *(He laughs)* I want the old days back! Where are they? Where have they gone? I mean, the old days were great— weren't they, Robert? Oh yes, the old old days were *wonderful* days! And they were better for me—I mean, personally, you see, they were much better for me.

ROBERT

Yes—of course—

DICK

And you know—you remember—I loved being an actor! It was nice, being an actor! What a fun way to live! I loved it, really. I know, I know, I wasn't that good, but—

ROBERT

What? You were!

DICK

Oh no, no—

17

ROBERT

Of course you were.

(A pause.)

DICK

Well—*you* didn't think so.

ROBERT

What? I did!

(Dick is silent. He pointedly looks off into the distance.)

Oh come on, Dick. What? I did.

(Dick is silent.)

What are you—? —You don't mean—my stupid play? But that—that was—that had nothing to do with me. I—

(Dick suddenly stares offstage and points.)

DICK

Oh my God, am I hallucinating? Oh my God! Isn't that—

(Robert too now sees the group offstage.)

ROBERT

Oh! Yes! Yes, that's Bill—

DICK

My God! Bill!

ROBERT

And Ted—and Annette—

DICK

And Tom, of course—the magnificent Tom—but this—
(Laughing) —this—this reminds me of one of those nights
when you sleep in an overheated room—you know?—and
you dream you're surrounded by every horrible person
you've ever met in your life!— *(Laughing)* —Or you know,
to put it a bit differently, *(Laughing)* you're surrounded by all
your favorite people, and you're absolutely thrilled! *(Laughing. He waves and shouts to the group)* Hello, everybody! *(He
stares for a moment, then turns back to Robert)* My God, what's
the matter? Don't they recognize me?

ROBERT

Well—er—you do look somewhat different, Dick.

DICK

Hey—so do you. A bit less tidy around the edges, perhaps?
(Confidingly) Say, by the way, how have things gone, over all
these years, with your—er—you know, the problem you had?

(Robert looks blank.)

The special problem you had? You know, the problem you
had about *hating* people? I remember you used to have a terrible problem about hating people. Remember? You couldn't
control it at all. Some of us—well, some of us fell victim to
that. You know, you couldn't control your hatred towards
certain people . . .

ROBERT

I don't remember that.

DICK

Oh, come on—you *must* remember hating me, at least. I mean, that was why I didn't get that part in *Midnight in a Clearing*. Of course I *wasn't* very good, I *wasn't* a good actor, I know that now, but that wasn't the reason I didn't get the part. I didn't get the part because you kept telling Bill, "I'm sorry, I hate him. I can't help it. I happen to hate him, and I don't want him around me." *(He laughs)* I mean, at least that's apparently what you kept telling Bill—I mean, you know, you hated me personally, you refused to let him hire me—you put your foot down—or anyway that's what Bill told me you'd said—I *assumed* it was true . . .

ROBERT

Dick, seriously—

DICK

I mean, I *wasn't* a good actor, but the funny thing was—and I've always thought this—the funny thing was that I think I would have been good in *that part*, because I felt I was sort of right for it, you see. I had an insight into it. And I felt that *Bill* was rather on my side about that, he did say that of all the people you were thinking about, I seemed to be the one who was most likely to capture some of the less obvious sides of the character, you see, the special secrets he had, the more interesting parts of the *writing*, quite frankly. I don't know— I'm just saying that that was how Bill seemed to feel, and he was *probably* wrong, but who knows, maybe I *could* have brought something to it that Tom in a way couldn't quite pull off, or didn't pull off, or—I don't know. It's possible. You know. I'm just saying—it's possible. It's possible. It's not *im*-possible. I mean, I might have cut to the heart of it, you see, in a way that was outside of Tom's range, in a way. I don't know. Who knows? I mean, you know, Tom was excellent. He did an excellent job. I'm just saying, it was a possibility.

ROBERT

A lot of time has passed, Dick. You're talking about—

DICK

Oh. I'm sorry, I thought you brought it up. I thought you were the one who brought up the subject. But you know, it's possible it was me. Maybe somehow I sensed that you were thinking about it, I don't know, so I somehow mentioned it. I mean, you know, it's not as if I'm constantly brooding about it.

ROBERT

No . . . Good . . . I mean, you had a wonderful career, Dick. I certainly wouldn't know why you'd—

DICK

(Laughs) No really, I'm sorry. You see, that's my problem. I keep talking about things that come into my head. Because my— *(Coughs, chokes)* —my life— *(Chokes)* —my—

ROBERT

Are you all right?

DICK

Yes, yes, I'm fine. *(Gasps)* The *beating* had some consequences, obviously, in some of the parts of my— *(Chokes)* —You know, when I—er— *(Chokes)*

ROBERT

Look, I realize this must be a terrible time for you, I—

(Dick subsides into a chair and begins to shiver, then shake, almost as if he's convulsing slightly.)

I mean—for God's sake—don't try to talk—can I get you something? A glass of water? I—

(As Robert starts to head offstage, Ted, Annette, Bill, and Tom come in and joyfully embrace him, shouting, "Robert! Robert!" and improvising greetings. Dick continues to cough and shake.)

(To the others) Look, I was just getting a glass of water for—

(He finds a pitcher and a glass and pours some water. The others notice Dick and go toward him. Dick's tremors increase.)

BILL

Good Lord . . . What's going on? Can we—

(Dick's tremors moderate a bit.)

DICK

No, no—I'm fine.

(Bill recognizes Dick.)

BILL

Dick! Dick! My God . . .

DICK

Yes, I know. I've gained weight.

(They all gather around Dick. Robert tries to give Dick water, but Dick rebuffs it.)

TED

Dick, this is incredible . . .

ANNETTE

Hi, Dick.

DICK

Oh my God—Ted? Annette? So you're here too? I can't believe it . . .

(Dick fades out, seems to be unconscious, except that he keeps moving vaguely and making odd sounds.)

ANNETTE

Is he all right?

TED

He looks like he's having a seizure of some kind . . .

BILL

No, no, he must be drunk or something . . .

23

(Nellie and Jane come in. They don't notice Dick.)

NELLIE

(To Robert) This is a miracle. It's so wonderful to see you, Mr. Robert. We've missed you so much.

JANE

Yes—you're looking well . . .

ROBERT

Nellie—Jane—

(Dick starts coughing again and trembling more visibly.)

TOM

Nellie—er—what's the story with Dick? Is he all right?

NELLIE

Is he all right?

TOM

I mean, is Dick a member here? Is he—I mean—do you know what's wrong with him? Is he ill, or—

NELLIE

Well, he's been a member here longer than practically anyone, you see. And he's been beaten up rather frequently. So this is the result. We've given him a room upstairs until he feels a bit better.

(They all stand around Dick. His coughing and trembling begins to lessen.)

Well, you see, we do have two or three rooms upstairs that we give to people who need them. I mean, I do know how to put a basic bandage on a wound. And we make a very nice breakfast for them, and we give them a cold lunch—very simple— But the rooms are quite sunny, and they can look out the window and see a bit of sky and even some greenery—some grass and trees. It's very quiet up there. And in the afternoon we always have tea and some rather nice cakes. So yes, we do take care of certain people occasionally, when someone needs to be kept cozy and comfortable.

ROBERT

My God, it sounds like heaven. Can I move in?

(They all laugh.)

TOM

So the old Talk House has taken on a few new functions, it seems—is that right, Nellie?

NELLIE

Oh no, no, I wouldn't say that. But everyone—please—tell Jane what you'd like to drink. We have all the old cocktails— and a few new ones!

(Jane begins to take drink orders and serve drinks. Improvised dialogue about the drinks can overlap with the written dialogue. After being served an initial drink by Jane, everyone goes up to the bar at different times to refill their drinks.)

TED

And won't you have something to drink, Nellie?

NELLIE

Well, no, I won't. When we have guests, you know, I only drink my Emerald Surprise.

(Nellie pours herself a green liquid from a distinctive green bottle on the bar.)

TED

It looks delicious.

BILL

And of course you still have all your special snacks, don't you?

NELLIE

Oh, we certainly do. We still have all the old snacks, and of course occasionally we do add something new, but, you know, the old "Talk House style" hasn't changed a bit . . . For better or worse. I mean, obviously we've fallen out of fashion to some extent . . .

ROBERT

Oh?

NELLIE

Oh yes, we're certainly out of fashion. We certainly are. You know, there was a time when we used to need three cooks working in the kitchen! On most nights, really, this place would be so full of people that we couldn't close till three in the morning!

ROBERT

Of course, yes . . .

TED

Yes, everyone I'd ever known in my life would end up here on one night or another.

NELLIE

Well, it's different now. I mean, people do still come, but the daring outfits people used to wear—that's all gone— and oh my God, when I think of the romances that flow- ered inside these walls back then—the hands touching under the table—no, no . . . I mean, where are all the lively people? Maybe they're somewhere. They're not here.

BILL

Really . . . Yes . . .

NELLIE

And I mean, we certainly don't get to see any of *you* very often, now do we, Mr. Bill?

BILL

Well—I mean—

NELLIE

Why *is* that, Mr. Robert, if I may ask? Can you tell me the reason, since we're speaking so frankly?

27

ROBERT

Oh, there's no reason at all. You know, the lure of the new. We've been seduced by ridiculously expensive, flashier places, to be absolutely frank. I mean, speaking for myself.

TOM

Yes, it's the same with me, I'd have to confess.

BILL

Some of us have to go to bed at night. It's not as if we're singing songs somewhere else.

ANNETTE

And some of us have to deal with the exciting challenge of having no money. I'd love to have somebody else cook my dinner. I don't enjoy cooking, I'm not a great cook, I'd come here every night if I could afford it.

NELLIE

Well, our little club is offering some pretty good deals these days.

ANNETTE

Yes, but you see, my club's more exclusive. No one can join but me.

TED

Oh yes, the one-member club is the latest thing. Mine is *so* nice and snug. And you see, there are very few disturbances in my club. No one makes a scene, no one complains about the food, no one hangs around too late. And it's terribly informal. I mean, I can walk around in my underwear, and no one complains.

NELLIE

(To Ted) No, I do understand. It's just sad to see so little of you, dear. *(To Tom)* I mean, you're the only one I see all the time, Mr. Tom—I mean, on my screen. You've kept us all laughing through good times and bad, as people say. I used to watch old episodes of your show practically every night when my dear, sick mother was in the hospital—it was very comforting.

TOM

Damn, it's nice to hear you say that, Nellie. I'm pretty tired of the old show myself, by now, to be absolutely frank, as I was saying to Robert only yesterday, I think.

ROBERT

Yes, you did say that yesterday. And the day before. And the day before that. And the day before that.

(They both laugh. Dick's eyes open.)

NELLIE

Don't you ever stop doing your show, Mr. Tom! I don't think we'd survive.

TOM

I really appreciate your saying that, Nellie.

ROBERT

Yes, thank you, Nellie. You know, the truth is, you can honestly go into the studio and work yourself sick every day, week after week, and at the same time you really can actually forget that there's anyone out there watching the damned thing—that's honestly the truth.

NELLIE

Oh we're watching, all right. It's a wonderful show.

(Dick rouses himself. He seems to have recovered.)

DICK

Yes, it's very well written, and it's very well done. And you make me laugh, Tom, you really do. It's a fine show.

TOM

Well, so was yours, Dick.

DICK

It's kind of you to say that, Tom.

(Dick walks off.)

NELLIE

And now *speaking* of things we love, isn't it about time for you all to do another play? We need more plays!

TOM

Well, it takes a lot of effort to put on a play . . .

ROBERT

And our last attempt wasn't *entirely* successful, one has to admit . . .

NELLIE

Oh, those critics were idiots! They didn't know what they were talking about. For God's sake. It was a fantastic play. "And as I stepped into the darkened meadow, I heard a cry, and there I saw a man no bigger than a newborn doe . . ."

ROBERT

Good Lord! You remember those lines? . . .

NELLIE

Of course of course! But why don't you all do more theater these days? I don't understand . . .

ANNETTE

Oh, it isn't us. I mean, we don't do theater because the theater isn't there. It's gone, you see.

BILL

There's no more theater.

TED

It sort of got very quiet, and then it just wasn't there at all.

TOM

People stopped going to see plays. They just gave up.

31

ANNETTE

The plays got too sad. They were sad and miserable.

BILL

And the erotic element wasn't very nice.

ANNETTE

People didn't want to be reminded of things like that, so they stayed at home, and so all the people who used to work in the theater went into all sorts of different fields.

ROBERT

So the theater is gone, but there are new things now. Change is inevitable, everything changes, things change, that's the rule of life. The world moves on.

TOM

The world moves on. It certainly does. The world moves on. And I mean, by the way, speaking of that, what do you think about all these elections, Nellie? Bill and I were just talking about that. What's going on with this crazy number of elections we're having? They're just too frequent—don't you think so?

NELLIE

Oh yes, I agree. Once a year was more than enough for me—every three months is almost irritating. And I mean, Ackerley almost always wins anyway, you know, almost always, and he's had the job for much too long, anyway, I would say.

TOM

Bill and I were saying the very same thing.

BILL

You know, I like Ackerley, and I like Rodman—I've voted for Rodman more than once—

NELLIE

Of course, so have I. I mean, they're both good people— though I don't find either of them particularly brilliant, if you really want to know . . .

BILL

Brilliant—well—

TOM

I mean, Ackerley's quite a *remarkable* man, he—

TED

Yes, I suppose . . .

NELLIE

(To Tom) Have you met him, Mr. Tom?

(During the following, Jane and Nellie begin to bring out and serve snacks. There can either be a lot of snacks or not so many, and everyone can either be seated at a table or not. Quiet murmuring about the serving of the snacks can also be improvised. As the guests talk, Nellie and Jane keep the room tidy, occasionally refill drinks, supply food.)

TOM

Oh yes, of course, a number of times.

NELLIE

And?

TOM

Well, he's very charming, very clever of course. I like him
very much. You know, he's very knowledgeable about film,
among other things. He has a secret taste for Korean films—
you'd be surprised. He knows the names of Korean actresses,
I'm serious.

NELLIE

I had no idea . . .

*(Dick wanders back in and sits quietly at some distance from the
others.)*

TOM

And on the subject of dogs, my God—

NELLIE

Yes?

TOM

You know I saw him about a year ago at some ceremony or
other, and I mentioned something about my pugs. Well, it
turns out his knowledge of the origins of dog breeds is absolutely extraordinary. And he has all sorts of theories about
the transmission of various characteristics having to do with,

you know, why spaniels have such tranquil personalities and things like that. So he's pretty impressive, he really is. But of course Rodman's a very nice fellow as well. He has some pretty strict principles, obviously, as everyone knows, but he's remarkably friendly and sincere, and he really likes a lot of people whom he actually despises, if you know what I mean.

BILL

Well yes, that's true . . . And I mean, of course they're both well-meaning people, and they're bright and competent, I know all that, but in a way I've gotten fed up with both of them, really, because I just can't stand that "Program of Murdering," it gets bigger every year—I mean, I think it's awful, and I don't know why they—

TOM

Well, to some extent I think they got into all that because they found it attracted an awful lot of voters—I mean, that's all very popular in the rural areas, isn't it.

BILL

Well, I'm sure it is, but you can't just snuff out this enormous number of lives because people in the rural areas find it—because they find it somehow—

ANNETTE

Well, it isn't really an enormous number of lives.

BILL

It—what?

ANNETTE

It isn't an enormous number of lives.

BILL

It isn't?

ANNETTE

Well, not compared to the number of lives that are lost in a war.

BILL

Really. You see, to me it seems like an enormous number.

ANNETTE

Well, it's a serious matter if a policy leads to the loss of life, of course it's a serious matter, but policies that govern the regulation of various drugs cost lives, policies that govern the regulation of games cost lives . . .

BILL

But the Program of Murdering is growing faster than any other program, it—

TOM

Well, I think Annette's just saying that if there *were* no such program, then we—we might be involved in—

ANNETTE

Let's put it this way. It happens to be necessary, it can't really be avoided, and so we shouldn't get obsessed about it. It's like

36

something one does behind one's own back, so to speak—
like something slightly unpleasant that one does with one's
ass once a day or so without paying it really a lot of attention.

TOM

Well, that's—

BILL

So what are you saying? I'm not—

ANNETTE

I'm saying, you know, we go about our lives every day—we
go to work, we talk, we drink glasses of wine—and every
once in a while, occasionally even in the middle of dinner,
we feel the need to go into the nearest bathroom and use our
asses to get rid of some waste. And we barely even give it
a moment's thought. So I mean, you know, pardon me, but
I'm making an analogy between dropping some waste into
the toilet, you see, and dropping a few small bombs onto certain targets, you know, dropping some rather small bombs
onto certain people who pose a threat to us, all rather casual,
and then you wash your hands and return to the table, and
there you have your Program of Murdering. It takes very
little time, it's barely noticeable, it's something you could say
that everyone does, and in the context of our lives and all the
things we do, it's rather trivial.

(A pause.)

ROBERT

Very few people do use the bathroom in the middle of dinner.

TOM

(Ignoring Robert; to Annette) No, I do understand all that, certainly, but you see, *my* problem is just that I always worry, can we really be sure that we're murdering the right people? That's what worries me.

ANNETTE

Well, we're getting awfully good at determining that. We really are. An incredible amount of effort goes into that.

BILL

Oh come on, Annette. How do you know? I mean, how have you become such an authority on this? What makes you think you know anything about it?

ANNETTE

Well—I've done it, darling.

(A pause.)

ROBERT

Oh—

TOM

Really—

BILL

What have you done?

ROBERT

You've done—?—what?

ANNETTE

The private tailoring business is not what it used to be, in case you don't happen to know that, Bill. Yes, I'm not *ashamed* of it—quite the contrary. Quite the contrary! Of *course* I've done targeting. Of *course* I have, like half the people you know.

BILL

Targeting? Are you serious?

TOM

Is that right.

ROBERT

You target people.

ANNETTE

I study lists of people, and I select the individuals who need to be killed. And I'm delighted to tell you that it brings me a paycheck, and the amazing thing is that my paycheck arrives with complete regularity. It's a small check, obviously, but they never say, "Oh, I'm so sorry, we can't pay you this week, but we promise to pay you next week for sure."

BILL

Well, you know, this is a surprise, it really is. And—er—and you really shouldn't say—you shouldn't just say you've done targeting "like half the people you know," because, with all respect, the people *I* happen to know have *not* done it, I'm very sorry.

ANNETTE

Well, yes, they have.

BILL

Oh come on, Annette, that's really absurd. I mean, I'm surprised *you've* done it, and I don't happen to know other people who've done it!

ANNETTE

Excuse me—you do.

BILL

Well, who are you talking about? You keep—

TED

Oh for God's sake, Bill. Don't pretend to be such an idiot. Annette's done it, I've done it. A lot of people you know have done it. It's not some strange mysterious activity. It's a very simple, mechanical process, and that's all. Don't you know that children are being trained to do it in school?

BILL

What?

TOM

Are they?

TED

I'm not saying they're actually doing it, but yes, in certain schools they're receiving training in targeting as part of the curriculum.

(Jane goes out.)

BILL

Well—

TED

Bill, it's a very simple, mechanical process. It's not as if we're looking at somebody's photograph and sort of saying, "Hm, I don't like the expression on that guy's face, I think he should be killed." It's not like that. We're targeting people who present a serious danger. We're applying a list of criteria to people. We're—

BILL

What kind of—?—

TED

And there are certain people who meet the criteria—A, B, C, D, it's a very long list—and if they meet the criteria, you can be goddamned sure that these are people who are dangerous to us. In other words, these are people who would like to harm us.

BILL

And those are the ones you feel should be killed?

TED

That's what I'm saying. What are you trying to ask me, Bill? I don't understand.

BILL

When they meet the criteria, they ought to be killed.

TED

Yes, because they would like to harm us. What are you trying
to—

BILL

What—

TED

Do you want to be harmed?

BILL

No! I don't! But how are you defining—I mean—

TED

Look, Bill, I mean, you're giving me the sense that you find
this all just terribly distasteful. You're *recoiling*, somehow.
I mean, you seem very dubious about whether it's true that
there are people out there who would like to harm us. Well,
I can assure you, there are. Believe it or not, there are people
out there who don't like you, and they don't like me. And—

BILL

Yes, but I mean, isn't there a sort of rather important distinc-
tion to be drawn between—I mean—a person who might
possibly harbor certain negative thoughts about us, on the
one hand, and—

TED

Of course there is. That's the crucial—that's it!—that's
the crucial element of accurate targeting! You don't seem
to understand that there are people who've already thought

about this. There are psychologists and sociologists who've devoted their lives to this—they've done very, very exhaustive studies analyzing the precise difference between— between some guy who's sitting in some miserable room thinking resentful thoughts about us because life hasn't met his expectations, on the *one* hand, and on the *other* hand, some *other* guy sitting in a *similar* room, who may outwardly *seem* to be just like the first guy, but—

BILL

And by the way, where are these people? Are they—I mean, are we talking about people who live in—I mean, where are we talking about now?

ANNETTE

Where?

BILL

(To Annette) I mean, you say you targeted people. Where were they, exactly?

ANNETTE

Well, in my case, they were in Malaysia.

BILL

So I mean, tell me about them. What sort of people were they? Were they businessmen? Were they—?—

ANNETTE

A majority of them made a living by herding sheep. When they weren't being trained in the use of explosives.

BILL

But I mean, if they were being trained in the use of explosives, did their training in explosives become their permanent job at some point, or did they just study explosives occasionally? Was it a weekend thing, or—I mean, were they in
an *army*, or—?—

ANNETTE

I really don't know, and the questions you're asking are completely irrelevant, because the crucial element in determining whether a person is going to harm you is not how many
lessons in explosives he's had, it's the type of feeling he has
about you. That's the thing I need to know.

(Nellie is serving more food.)

TED

We're trying to find the people who have the potential to
harm us. And they have the *potential* to harm us because
they'd *like* to harm us.

BILL

Yes, but you see, putting people's feelings to one side for just
a moment, I mean, how do you know that some person who
lives thousands of miles away from you will ever even get
close enough to you to harm you at all?

TED

I'm not saying he'll harm *me*, I'm saying he'll harm *us*. And
I'm not saying he'll do it all by himself, maybe he'll help
some of his friends to do it. He'll do whatever he's able to

do, and what that might be, I can't possibly know. What I *do* know is that he happens to be a member of that particular category of people who would like to harm us, and so if we get rid of him, and we get rid of all the other people in that particular category, then there won't be anyone left who would like to harm us, and so no one will harm us. Is that really so hard to understand?

(A pause. Nellie offers a tentative thought.)

NELLIE

You have to wonder, What would happen if the people we're targeting were ever to learn our techniques—and start going after us? What if everybody—started targeting everybody? And little bombs were flying between everybody and everybody? . . .

ROBERT

Well . . .

ANNETTE

(Ignoring Nellie) And by the way—by the way, the things we've done have really made a difference. I mean, we happen to be winning. People are worrying much much less. I mean, do you remember that day five years ago when there was that peculiar gas floating across the river, and people thought it might be some form of mustard gas? Did that by any chance frighten you, Bill?

BILL

Yes, it did, I was very frightened.

45

ANNETTE

I remember the way I felt when I heard about that gas—the way I was shaking with fear, I was actually *sick*. Well, things like that aren't happening now. We're all less afraid—less afraid of all of those people, because—

BILL

And—pardon me if I'm going around in circles here—*why*, did you say, do all these people have this desire to harm us?

TED

Why do they—?—

BILL

Why do they want to harm us, did you say?

TED

I *didn't*—I didn't *say* why. Who *cares* why?

BILL

Well, one does have a certain curiosity about it.

ANNETTE

Well, darling, I mean, if you walk out of your apartment onto the street one day, and there's a man on the sidewalk firing shots at you, I'm not sure it makes sense to sort of stand there musing about what particular problems in the poor man's life might have led him to become a homicidal maniac. I think you'd want to hide behind a car or something. You know, find at least a temporary solution to the problem at hand.

TED

Or a permanent solution—kill the guy.

BILL

Yes, that would settle it.

(A pause. Bill glances around the room.)

(To Ted and Annette, chuckling) You know, you all honestly remind me of that character on Leonard Manville's old show who used to shoot some stranger in a bar practically every other episode.

TED

You mean, the guy they called Porky Horowitz? Thanks a lot there, Bill.

ANNETTE

Yes—very flattering.

ROBERT

Oh, Porky wasn't really such a bad fellow. He just had a rather low tolerance for people who were rude.

TOM

Quite understandable.

DICK

Say, incidentally, did any of you hear what happened to Daphne Albright last week?

ROBERT

No. What?

DICK

(To Robert) God, what log have *you* been sleeping under?

ROBERT

Well—what happened to her?

DICK

Well, she was having dinner over at *Le Grand Plaisir*—

TED

I can't *stand* that place.

DICK

—and she *died* there. They say she kept getting up to use the bathroom, and then at a certain point, she came back from the bathroom, and she started making these weird noises, these weird sounds like "Erk erk erk"—"erk erk erk"—and then—she died!

ANNETTE

Died?! What? *(Everyone reacts)* That's just impossible!

BILL

But that sounds like exactly what happened to Nestor Crawley. The bathroom thing, and then those sounds—

TED

Oh my God—Crawley—I'd *forgotten* that!

TOM

Crawley, of *course*—I was there that night, at Raymond's, I was just coming in for a drink after the show, and the police cars were just pulling out of the driveway with Nestor's corpse! God help us. What?—have we been phasing in some new technique?

DICK

It's hardly new, dear, it's been around for years. It's a bit like arsenic. Tiny gray little pellets—no taste at all. Your friend drops two or three of them into your drink, and bam!—half an hour later you're *gone*, that's *it*.

BILL

Good Lord . . . The Horrible Crawley . . .

TED

Well, he *was* horrible, but still, that's an awful way to go, I think.

BILL

Oh, it could be worse.

(A slight pause. Nellie goes out.)

DICK

Do you know?—I always think one should reflect very carefully before one makes a remark like that. I mean, you casually say something like "it could be worse." But to me, you see—well, I happen to be quite a superstitious person, and as a superstitious person I can't help but believe that if you casually make light of some particular form of human suffer-ing—a disease, say, or some type of calamity, or, you know, as in this case, a manner of dying—then quite possibly that form of suffering will take offense at it somehow and will somehow return to make you regret your remark.

(A slight pause.)

ANNETTE

I think—I think that's a terrible thing to say.

(A slight pause.)

DICK

Well—fine, then. I take it back. *(He stands up and starts to leave)*

ANNETTE

(To Dick, as he leaves) We're trying to have a pleasant evening!

DICK

Annette, sweetheart, Daphne Albright was trying to have a pleasant evening. Nestor Crawley was trying to have a pleas-ant evening. They just happened to be people who began to behave in a way that was *(He mimes odd animal-like behavior, as before)* "grr—grr—grr," for which they were rewarded in an unpleasant way. And that's all. I think I'll go and help Nel-lie in the kitchen, excuse me.

(Dick leaves. They all watch him go.)

TOM

Oh my God, he's become a—a poisonous snake! I can't believe it. He used to be such a sweet little fellow.

TED

He used to curl up on my piano bench and listen to me play— like a little cat.

BILL

Horrible. He's dreadful.

(Jane wanders in.)

ANNETTE

Jane, Dick's become an absolute horror. A horror! How can you let him stay here overnight?

JANE

Oh my God, what's he been doing?

ANNETTE

Oh nothing, nothing. He's just been telling us about the deaths of some awful people we used to know, when we're trying to have a pleasant evening . . . Disgusting—it's disgusting! He seems to be completely out of control . . .

JANE

I know, I know . . . We've done our best to—

ANNETTE

Well, it's not working!

JANE

Oh my God . . .

ANNETTE

The tone of his voice—it was as if he was enjoying it—and he was telling us that people we know are being poisoned—their drinks are being poisoned—

TOM

Well, Dick isn't your fault, Jane. For goodness sake.

ROBERT

No, of course he isn't.

(A silence.)

ANNETTE

He's just become such a vicious person. I just— *(She falls silent)*

TOM

But anyway, Jane, how are you doing these days? Why don't you sit down with us here and tell us what you've been up to for all these years.

JANE

Oh no, no. I really shouldn't.

TOM

Now, don't be absurd. We'd love to hear all about you—we all would.

JANE

Really?

ROBERT

Absolutely.

JANE

Well, all right then—thank you very much. *(She sits down)* My, what comfortable chairs we have here! *(They all laugh)*

TOM

So tell us everything, Jane. Surely you haven't been sitting here at The Talk House for all this time, have you?

JANE

No, not really. I've just been back for a year or so, actually.

TOM

So tell us about your adventures, then.

JANE

Oh, it's a pretty long story. It's been quite a few years since I've seen you all. You know, I was on that show *Mouse Chatter* for quite a while—I mean, I only had a very small part, but that was great . . .

ANNETTE

You mean with Heidi Jones?

JANE

Yes, Heidi Jones!

BILL

At first we all found those crazy Heidi mannerisms so endearing, didn't we, but after a year or two it was more like, For God's sake, will you stop *doing* that? *(Chuckling)* And I *didn't* like that young boy on the show.

JANE

Sam? You didn't?

BILL

No! I didn't! He was weak—he was self-pitying—he was just revolting, really—I mean, he was such a worm-like, whiny, creepy little thing . . . and he had *no* personality—none at all . . .

TED

Bill—please—maybe Jane was a friend of the boy . . .

BILL

Well, if he was your friend, I'm sorry, I'm sure in real life he was a very nice person, but he made my flesh crawl—

TOM

We hear you, Bill. No, my problem with the show was just with the writing. I mean, the stories were pointless. I'm not saying everything has to be *Atlantic History* or, you know, *Pills*— *(General chuckling)* —but you have to have some desire, when you're watching a show, to know what's going to be happening next. You have to at least be thinking, even if the subject is completely silly, "Oh, I wonder if she's going

to look in the drawer and find Fred's socks in there," or—
you know what I mean.

ANNETTE

It just wasn't funny enough, I always felt. Heidi Jones wasn't
funny.

ROBERT

Heidi Jones *was* funny when she did that short-lived thing
about all those nuns who drank too much. But when you have
people like Rick Hazelton and Harvey Knowles, who had no
qualifications whatsoever to be running a show, in charge
of things, naturally they hired the worst writers, the worst
directors—it's really a miracle it lasted as long as it did.

(A silence.)

TOM

(To Jane) So then what did you do when *Mouse Chatter* ended?

JANE

Oh, I did a couple of other shows that weren't that great, and
I did one or two plays. And then I went abroad for a while.
I worked as a murderer for the "Special Areas Project" for
three or four years, if you really want to know. Not very nice.

TOM

Oh, God. That's awful. Where did they send you? Nigeria?

JANE

Yeah, mostly Nigeria. They had me out in Indonesia for a
while—I don't know . . .

TED

Damn. Really. So, what did they have you doing, exactly?

JANE

Well, I stuck people with—you know—pins, I guess—I mean, I shouldn't laugh, because it was actually awful—but I scratched people, basically. In crowds, or sports events, or you know, mostly on the street. I'd scratch them, there'd be about two minutes where they'd feel sort of odd, supposedly, then they'd die, and of course by then I'd be far away.

ROBERT

Really. Just dreadful.

JANE

A few times I had to kill someone more directly—you know, when there was someone who wasn't really all that bad, but they still decided that they had to be killed, and they were basically giving them a painless end . . . You know, these were people who wouldn't be able to put up a fight—quite elderly people. I mean, I was basically the angel of mercy, or whatever you want to call it, so the person would usually just curl up into a ball and let me stick them. I wasn't great at it—you had to stick them in the right place, obviously, to be sure it was pain-less, and I was always nervous, I guess, so it wasn't always as easy as it sounds. But when they saw me coming, they knew I was going to be doing it nicely—as opposed to opening their door one day and seeing *Ray* standing there—do you remember Ray, that guy who used to work at the coffee shop next door, with the bright red shirts?

ANNETTE

Oh, yes . . . Ray . . .

JANE

You know, I did it the nice way, and they always used Ray to do it the bad way—you know, the horrible way—with—

ROBERT

Please—don't tell us—we don't want to know!

(They all laugh.)

JANE

Anyway, eventually I just decided to come back home and work for Nellie again . . .

TOM

Much nicer.

JANE

And Africa's hard—you know, the food isn't great, most people are starving, it's really bad.

ROBERT

Right, right.

(A slight pause.)

TOM

You know, Nigeria's one of the worst territories in the world for our show, actually. Almost nobody watches it there. I'm not even sure they're still showing it there.

JANE

No, no, they wouldn't like it there at all. Definitely not. Different sense of humor. Completely different.

ROBERT

Actually, we are still shown in Nigeria. I mean, to tell you the truth, Nigeria honestly isn't as bad for us as it might be, compared to a lot of other places. I mean, Luxembourg, for example, has completely died on us.

ANNETTE

Really. How strange.

JANE

You know, I have a friend in Luxembourg, and I'll bet none of you can guess what their *favorite* show is.

BILL

Their favorite show—?—

ANNETTE

William and Mike?

JANE

No, no, you'll never guess! And I mean, I'm talking about an *incredible* success. The most successful show.

TED

The Life of Horace?

(A pause.)

JANE

The Ocean of Blood.

(Everyone exclaims, except Robert.)

BILL

No—I don't believe it.

ROBERT

No, Bill, you see, you don't understand. I knew exactly what Jane was going to say. *The Ocean of Blood* is becoming a phenomenon! It's just amazing.

ANNETTE

Are you talking about that insane show that nobody watches—

ROBERT

Yes!

ANNETTE

—with people who've just been—shot or something?—

ROBERT

Yes!

ANNETTE

—the "wound show"??—

59

ROBERT

Yes, that's the show, and no one understands the—certain countries just seem to have become addicted to it—I mean, Luxembourg, Singapore, the South Sea Islands—oh my God! It's their favorite show! . . . You know, here, the people who make that show are completely unknown. I mean, their office is just down the street from ours—and it's the most run-down, awful, shabby little *hut*, almost, with an overgrown, ugly little lawn out in front. And the host of the show, Bob Hatfield, he just walks down the street there and goes in the door, and nobody knows who the hell he is. But if Hatfield were to walk down the street in—in—in Bangladesh—well, he couldn't *walk* down the street in Bangladesh, there'd be such a mob—

TED

Bob Hatfield the singer?

ROBERT

He's not spending very much time on his singing these days, I can tell you that.

TED

But you mean to say, it *is* the same guy?

ROBERT

Oh yes, he used to be with that group—you know, with those people in little vests with those horrible beards—

TED

I'm telling you, bad singers can turn out to be the nastiest people on earth when they stop singing. I could give you a list.

BILL

Elaine Morddren.

TED

Elaine Morddren. One of the worst people on the planet today.

ANNETTE

Ethel Hardwick.

TOM

I will never forget the photograph of Ethel Hardwick when they raided her house and found all those cats—

ANNETTE

Oh, *don't!*—please—

TOM

I honestly hadn't realized cats could look like that—their bodies were *flat*—they looked like sort of giant furry tadpoles or something . . .

BILL

I'd just about managed to *forget* that photograph. Thank you, Tom.

TOM

Those poor cats . . .

TED

Bad singers, I'm telling you . . .

(A slight pause. Nellie and Dick come in carrying a cake. Everyone exclaims and gathers around the cake. Annette reads what's written on it.)

ANNETTE

"Midnight in a Clearing with Moon and Stars" . . .

BILL

Oh Nellie, really, that's fantastic.

ROBERT

That's just beautiful, Nellie. Just amazing.

NELLIE

Now, you cut the cake, Mr. Robert. I hope you still like cake.

ROBERT

Oh God help me, I do.

(Improvised words of appreciation as they pass around and taste the cake.)

NELLIE

Now, I think someone should read at least a few words from the play just to mark the occasion, as that's why you're all here—don't you agree, Mr. Robert?

ROBERT

Er—I'm not absolutely sure I *do* agree, Nellie—I—er—

NELLIE

Well, we've kept a copy in the library, of course. *(She shows it)* Now come along, Mr. Tom—please, for me—read us the speech about the bowl of raspberries. It's such a wonderful speech.

TOM

Oh no no no, I honestly can't.

ANNETTE

Oh come on, Tom. We'd love to hear it.

TOM

Good, but please don't ask *me*, because I haven't looked at that script in ten years, and I'm the world's worst reader, as Robert can tell you. It's my greatest weakness, really. I'd only embarrass myself and humiliate Robert. Really, I can't.

TED

So—the author himself will have to read.

ROBERT

I'm afraid that out of respect for the serious writer I used to be, I'm going to have to gracefully decline.

(Nellie, Jane, Ted, and Bill groan.)

BILL

Well, that's awful. Really.

JANE

Well—what about you, Dick?

DICK

What do you mean, what about me?

JANE

Why don't you read the speech?

(An uncomfortable silence.)

Come on, Dick. Nellie wants to hear it.

(A pause.)

DICK

Well, of course it's—it's awfully hard to measure these things, but that might be the worst idea I've heard this year. *(He stands up and starts to leave)* And as it's been a very long evening—

TOM

No, come on, Dick. It's a great idea. Really. It's fine. *(Including the group in a gesture)* You see? Look—they're absolutely clamoring for it.

TED

Absolutely.

(Jane leads Nellie, Ted, and Bill in a very brief chant.)

JANE, NELLIE, TED, AND BILL

Dick! Dick!

(Dick looks to Robert, who sort of smiles and shrugs.)

DICK

Well, in memory of a fine play, and of relationships that seemed at one time to hold much promise—I humbly—

(Nellie shows Dick the proper place in the script, Dick puts on his spectacles, moves into the light. Then he begins. He reads at an unrushed pace, clearly and well, looking around at the group at appropriate moments as if they were the other characters.)

"My friends, the king has spoken, so what can I add to what's been said? I love him and respect him, and it's been an honor to serve him during a moment such as this, when the fate of all we've stood for seemed to be in doubt, and we had no choice but to once again fight for it all with all our strength. Who would have dreamed that the Marmidons, over whom we've ruled for so long with wisdom and forbearance, would seek to plunge a knife into our breast? Or that our former friend Beltramidon would ever choose to betray our trust? No matter. Beltramidon lies now on the open slab of stone where I cut him down and ran him through with this humble blade with its wooden hilt. *(He raises his arm to indicate a sword)* Maggots run back and forth in the wounds I carved into his once-mighty body. And so tonight, we feast. In the black enormous pits outside, the golden antelopes have been placed on burning wood, covered in the skins of oranges and lemons, the heavy pungent herbs, the dark spices, cloves and berries, seeds and silver leaves carried on our bright white ships from far away. The meat of the golden antelope, friends, is known by tradition as the warrior's meat, yet our great poet has described it as 'so delicate, so sweet, and so tender that a small child can eat ten dishes of it'—and when the antelopes start to crackle on the flames and send forth into the air their delicious, penetrating scent, all the wild dogs for miles around will begin to rush towards us from every corner of the forest. The golden antelope, preeminently, of course, is the meat of triumph, and indeed we dare to say out loud, 'We've won, my friends. Against tremendous odds, we've won.' And what an honor for me to be offered this wonderful seat beside the glorious ruler who has secured for every one of us the hope of serenity and the treasures of the earth. And yet—forgive me, my king, and forgive me, friends: at this high moment, I beg to take my leave of you. My messengers tell me that across the lake in the land of Garmore, Queen Amendra finds herself threatened by a murderous tribe. She needs my help. So tomorrow morning, I must set out on another journey. And tonight, I must rest. I won't be staying for this marvelous feast. Instead, I'm going home to sit alone, by my own fire, and while all of you taste the intoxicating flesh of the golden antelope, I shall sit in my armchair with a bowl of raspberries, which will offer me more than sustenance enough to carry me happily into a long untroubled sleep. My dear companions—may you long continue to protect each other and take delight in each other, while I head out down my separate path."

(He looks up from the book. A brief silence.)

TED

Bravo. Marvelous.

(Everyone applauds.)

BILL

Yes indeed.

TOM

Damn—I never did the speech that well. Never.

JANE

Wonderful.

NELLIE

That brings it all back. Thank you so much, Dick.

(They sit in silence for a moment.)

DICK

Well, thank *you* all very much. You're being much too kind.

NELLIE

So. Shall we all have some coffee in the library?

(Nellie takes Dick's arm and leads everyone out, except for Rob-ert, who sits silently in his chair, sipping his drink, and Jane, who also remains behind. The group improvises comments as they leave. Robert is drunk, Jane not entirely sober either. They sit silently for a while.)

JANE

You know, I'm so worried about Dick. I don't know how much longer he's going to be allowed to live. *(Robert doesn't reply)* I mean, everyone's obviously incredibly tolerant of him because everyone really loved that show—it was such a great show—but at a certain point people do lose patience. I mean, everyone loved José's show too, but that only helped José up to a certain point.

ROBERT

José? What do you mean? What happened to José?

JANE

You don't know about it?

ROBERT

No—what do you mean?—

JANE

Well, you remember his best friend on the show was the neighbor, Ned, played by Renfield Matthews, who was also José's best friend in real life. Well, at a certain moment, Renfield just decided things had reached that point, and he got together this group of eight or ten people who'd all really loved José over all those years, and they went to his apartment, and well—they were really rough with him—you know, they cut him with knives, and I mean, very brutal cuts—

ROBERT

Oh—I hadn't—

JANE

—and then they took him out into the street in front of all of his neighbors and killed him.

ROBERT

Mm. My goodness. I didn't know. My God.

(They sit for a moment.)

So what did they finally do, shoot him?

JANE

Oh no, they hanged him. A terrible hanging, one of the worst.

(A silence. Robert keeps drinking steadily. Jane drinks along with him.)

ROBERT

You see, the difficulty about Dick is that Dick's show was so long ago that the younger people have never even *heard* of it, really. So, that's very unhelpful for Dick. And then, you see, unfortunately, *after* the show, Dick didn't *do* anything. By the time *we* all knew him, he was doing absolutely nothing, you see. I mean, I saw him once or twice in a Baldwin play—Bob Baldwin liked him—but very small parts, you know, nothing anyone would remember.

JANE

Right. Right.

ROBERT

And of course *my* problem with Dick was that I just never thought he was a very good actor, that was *my* problem from the very beginning. I mean, I hate to say it, because I know you're fond of him, but that's just the way I've always felt. Maybe it wasn't even his acting, I don't know. I just never enjoyed watching him, I'm sorry to say. He wasn't terribly likable, I always felt. I didn't particularly like him, you see.

JANE

Well, so much depends on the roles a person is offered. He—

(They fall into a long silence.)

I mean, obviously Dick was great on his show. He was so good as Chico! So the—

ROBERT

You see, I didn't think he was really that good. I'm sorry. I didn't. I mean, that—you know, that smile?—the "Chico smile"?—a lot of people found that charming, but I didn't, I must say, I thought it was just an awful smile. I mean, I suppose I'm saying that I happened to find him quite unappealing. Was it his appearance? His personality? I'm really not sure. I didn't enjoy him, I'd have to say.

JANE

Really. Really.

ROBERT

I mean, I know you like him, and I must say, he read that speech tonight very well, he did. I mean, he always had some sort of flair, of course. He had *something*. I'm not going to say he had no talent at all. But I just never thought he was a very good actor, and every time I watched that show, I honestly thought to myself, Well, I think this whole show would be a good deal funnier if they had someone else playing the part of Chico. Chico was always the weak link to me. Was Dick just not very believable somehow—or was it that the way he played him, Chico came off as not terribly sincere? I don't know. But I certainly didn't have that feeling of, "Yes, I really want to see more of this person. Watching him is fun, I love to watch him . . ."

JANE

Sure. I get it. *(Silence)* I mean, obviously Ralph Hirst was the one who *made* the show . . .

ROBERT

Sure, obviously. That's why people watched the show. Ralph and Hannah.

JANE

Right. Right.

(A silence.)

ROBERT

And I'm not sure I see the point of Nellie letting Dick stay here overnight at The Talk House. Do you? Seriously?

71

I mean, to be very honest—I worry about Nellie. It doesn't
look that great. Quite a few people would actually be repelled
by her doing that, you know.

JANE

By her doing what? You mean—

ROBERT

I mean, isn't it a statement? Like, "I think Dick is a person
whom I admire a great deal"? "And that's why I'm letting
him live at the club"?

JANE

Well, he doesn't live here. He's *staying* here for a few nights.
He doesn't *live* here.

ROBERT

He doesn't?

JANE

No!—

ROBERT

Well, where does he live then?

JANE

He *lives* in his own apartment.

ROBERT

So, Nellie's sort of hiding him, then, from the people who
beat him.

JANE

What?

ROBERT

Isn't that what you're saying?

JANE

Hiding him? You think she's hiding him? Look, she's taking care of him for a few days. No one's hiding anyone. He isn't hidden. He's right upstairs.

ROBERT

He's not living at his own address, is all I'm saying. A person's friends ought to be able to know where he is, and I wonder if his friends are aware that he happens to be here. That's the point I was trying to make—it's not all that complicated.

JANE

You mean—

ROBERT

See, if someone went to his apartment to find him, would there be any indication *there* that he happens to be *here*?

JANE

Well, I really don't know—I—

ROBERT

You see, that's my point. Because it's bad enough that he's here in the first place, but at least it should be clear that no one's keeping him here because they don't want people to know where he is. Do you know what I mean? So someone ought at least to leave some sort of very clear notification over at his apartment, wherever the hell that is, that would state very clearly that if you're looking for Dick, you can find him *here.*

JANE

Yes, that's a good idea. I see what you mean.

ROBERT

Because otherwise you run into the whole question of, Is Nellie "hiding" him?

JANE

Yes. Right.

ROBERT

Because that would be . . .

(A long silence. Jane speaks suddenly:)

JANE

All right, look, I'm sorry. I don't know what to say. I owe you an apology—I'm very sorry. Ted called, he said you all wanted to come over here—and I just thought, What a nice idea. Then I talked to Nellie—she was totally delighted. We just got terribly excited about the idea of Tom and you coming to the club. We just didn't think. The fact that Dick was here—we didn't even think about it. It didn't cross our minds. That may seem hard to believe, but it's the truth. We

behaved like idiots. Complete idiots. We should never have
let you come here. I'm sorry.

ROBERT

What are you——?——

JANE

Dick—you—in the same building—bad idea. Bad. Bad.

ROBERT

Don't be ridiculous—I'm—

JANE

You're an important person now, you're a public person. And
Tom, my God. I must have been completely out of my mind.
No one should see either of you here in the same building as
someone like Dick. I mean, that sort of thing wouldn't even
occur to Nellie. But I should have thought of it. It's completely my fault. It's—

ROBERT

Jane! Stop. You're almost insulting me now. I'm angry at
you for even *thinking* like this. It was *not* a mistake to have
us here. I'm not remotely concerned about being seen with
Dick. I'll walk down the street holding hands with Dick—
it doesn't bother me at all. Dick is a completely harmless,
pitiful person, and I'm sure that absolutely everybody knows
that, and I don't think for a minute that anyone's the least bit
worried about Dick.

JANE

His friends were worried—they beat him up. They—

ROBERT

Don't be silly—they gave him a warning. That means nothing. Just calm down. Everything's fine.

JANE

God, you're such a hypocrite. How disgusting. How nauseating. Yes, you're very dishonest—I remember that now.

ROBERT

Really? Do you? *(Pause)* You see, I only remember the physical things. I only remember the way it felt when we— Only the physical things. *(She is silent)* I said, I remember the physical things. You know—do you remember the—the physical—experiences we had? Do you remember the—sexual experiences—the—?—

JANE

No I don't.

ROBERT

You don't remember the times when we—?—

JANE

No I'm sorry, I don't.

ROBERT

You're lying, obviously.

JANE

Will you please stop it?

ROBERT

Because for me, you see, those were very important experiences. They were great, for me. Great. Extraordinary. As a matter of fact, when I think about my life, when I look back on—

JANE

For God's sake, will you please stop! It's been so many years—so many years since I've touched another person in that way! Oh my God, what possible benefit do you think I would get from thinking about all that? Do you think I would enjoy reminiscing about the times when I— *(She makes sounds of vomiting)* yuck!—yuck!—I feel so cold, I feel so sick—I'm so ready to die now, I am so ready, and I'm so bored, just waiting here month after month after month. Everybody else is begging to *live*, and I'm just begging, "Please get me out of here! Please! Please!" *(She laughs)* I'm totally involved in targeting, too, since everybody's talking about it. I thought it was supposed to be something absolutely secret—I guess I was wrong about that too, since it's apparently everybody's favorite topic of conversation. Yes, I do it every afternoon. I'm good at it, I guess. Every afternoon, all day Saturday, all day Sunday. It's totally sickening, it's totally boring, but Nellie can hardly pay me enough to cover my laundry, The Talk House is *broke*, I'm sorry to tell you. Of course I'd much rather be working on a show. I'd greatly prefer to be working on a show, but I've completely given up hope of that—I'm just not that funny, and I know that Rudolph doesn't find me attractive, and people used to tell me that Chuck *did* find me attractive, but I know that Chuck is nothing these days. Everyone says he's absolutely nothing.

ROBERT

Believe me, he's hardly doing any better than you are yourself. He's still sitting in that great big office, but he's utterly ignored, he can't help you *at all*, no matter *how* attractive he thinks you are.

JANE

Yes, that's what I just said.

ROBERT

Obviously *I* find you attractive, I always have, but I haven't been able to help you either, as you know very well. Rudolph simply won't—

JANE

It doesn't matter. I honestly don't care. I'm past all that now.

ROBERT

I would have liked to help you.

JANE

Right. You said that.

ROBERT

I think you're attractive, I think you're funny, and I honestly think you have talent as an actress. But you haven't been successful. It's terrible, really. And the murdering? The targeting? I hate to see you doing all that. I wish I could help you. I'm—I'm going to try to find you at least a small part, something that Rudolph wouldn't have to approve, because when it comes to Rudolph—

JANE

Don't bother. Seriously. Please—really, don't. You'll only make yourself look like an idiot, and I don't care how small the part is, Rudolph is going to step in and say no, so it won't do *me* any good, and it won't do *you* any good. No one can get me on any show at all, because fucking Rudolph doesn't like me, and that's that. If I were a bit funnier, I might have had a chance on Henry's show, because Henry liked me, but he told me flat out, "I really like you, but you're not quite funny enough to be on the show."

ROBERT

What an ass he is . . . I think you're *very* funny, and if I had control of *our* show, I swear to God—

JANE

The *only* thing I'd like, what would really please me, would be to be dead. *That* I would like. *That* I would *love*. That's what I think about. I want to be dead. I just think that all the time. "I want to be dead. I want to be dead."

(Pause.)

ROBERT

Do you seriously not remember the sexual thing?

79

JANE

Of course I remember it, but it doesn't make me happy to think about it now. It doesn't make me happy to think about playing in the park with my mother either. I don't want to think about things like that.

ROBERT

So you don't get pleasure from reliving the past? For me, that's the greatest pleasure in life. The past was great, and I love to think about it.

JANE

Well, you're very lucky.

ROBERT

Right. I'm sorry. *(Silence)* So when you say, "I'd like to be dead," I mean, do you— *(He falls silent)*

JANE

Yes, thanks for asking. No. I honestly don't know if I have what it takes to kill myself. I've thought it all through, all the different ways, I always imagine my instincts stopping me at the last moment . . . I don't want them to, but—

ROBERT

Right . . . Yes . . .

JANE

To be absolutely frank, what I dream about is the possibility of just walking out of The Talk House late one night, walking down the street, and without my even noticing it, having someone shoot me in the back of the neck. One shot in just the right place. Don't tell me yes or no, but if you happen to have the ability to make that happen, I'd be very grateful. *(A silence)* You know, they did that to Arnold. It happened to Arnold, and it happened to Winnie. And they finally did it to Allison, just last year. But obviously those are all pretty important people, you know, they're public figures, really. Arnold was, certainly. And I'm way down there. No one knows who I am, so it's hard for me to imagine that they'd—

ROBERT

Well, come on—I mean, you're not *completely* unknown. I mean, *Mouse Chatter* certainly had some kind of a following. There are definitely people who would know you from that.

(They sit silently for a while. Then Tom, Ted, Bill, Nellie, Annette, and Dick come in. A moment of silence.)

Nellie, you wonderful creature. We've had a great evening here, and we've all loved it.

NELLIE

Well, thank you, dear. You should come here more often, all of you, really.

TED

Nothing could be nicer, and we'll really try to.

NELLIE

(To Tom and Robert) And I'm sure some of the people from your show would like it here, too. Damn, I can't stop using the bathroom this evening, I'm so sorry.

(Nellie heads off to the bathroom. A silence.)

JANE

Nellie's right, absolutely. Some of the people from your show would have a *great* time here, I think. I mean, I've never met him, obviously, but wouldn't Timmy Barette, for example, like the atmosphere here? He seems like such an interesting, sort of refined person . . .

TOM

Well—

ROBERT

(Laughs harshly) Ha ha ha! Timmy Barette! Ha ha ha! A refined person! Ha ha ha! No, that's the misconception about Timmy Barette. Let me tell you, Timmy Barette is one of the filthiest barnyard *animals* you'll ever meet in your life. Ha ha ha! Timmy Barette is like a sort of tiny head sitting on top of—on top of an enormous dick! Ha ha ha ha! You do *not* want to bring Timmy Barette to dinner at The Talk House. Ha ha ha! You do *not*—

JANE

Oh, all right, stop! I guess—I guess—I guess Timmy Barette wasn't a great idea, was he?

(They all laugh.)

As everyone always says, you can never guess an actor's real personality from watching him play a character, can you?

BILL

Certainly not.

TED

No—

ANNETTE

No—not really—

ROBERT

No, you can't. You certainly can't. Except in the case of Tom, of course. Tony's a lovely guy, and so is Tom—aren't you, Tom?

TOM

I'm not sure, I can't remember anymore.

JANE

(Raising her glass to Tom) Let's all drink to a lovely guy!

TOM

Thank you, dear.

(The others murmur, "Hear hear." Nellie comes back from the bathroom.)

NELLIE

God— Please excuse me. *(To Dick)* Now, I was trying to think of that hilarious sound Daphne Albright made. Wasn't it sort of—"erk erk erk"—

DICK

Yes, exactly!

NELLIE

"Erk erk erk"— *(She laughs)* ha ha ha— "Erk erk erk"— "erk erk erk"—"erk erk erk"—

(Nellie wanders offstage.)

JANE

(Shouting to Nellie) I think we've got the idea, Nellie.

NELLIE

(Offstage) "Erk erk erk"—

(The lights flicker. Robert, Annette, Tom, Bill, Ted, Dick, and Jane look off toward Nellie. A long silence in which we hear Nellie:)

"Erk erk erk" . . . "erk erk erk" . . .

BILL

(To Jane) I think you should go see if something's wrong with her.

JANE

What do you mean?

TOM

I think we've exhausted her. *(To Annette)* Go and see if she's all right.

(Annette shrugs and heads out after Nellie. In the silence we still hear Nellie:)

NELLIE

(Offstage) . . . "erk erk erk" . . .

(Her sounds slowly diminish in volume. The lights sort of tremble and start to fade.)

ROBERT

(To the group) I'll tell you a story about Timmy Barette . . .

JANE

No, please *don't*. I'm very sorry I brought him up! Really. Please.

ROBERT

You don't want to hear it?

JANE

No, no, go ahead . . .

(We hear a faint cry from Nellie offstage.)

ROBERT

Well, the first part of the story isn't really that bad. I don't know if I'll even *tell* you the second part.

(Annette comes back in. Everybody looks at her.)

What?

(As Annette gestures offstage and tries to speak, the lights slowly flicker and then slowly go out.)

END